Secular Buddhism
An Introduction

Other Books by Jay N. Forrest

Practical Buddhism: Wisdom for Everyday Life

Humanism, God, and the Bible: An Ex-Pastor Examines the Evidence

Secular Buddhism
An Introduction

JAY N. FORREST

Secular Buddhism: An Introduction

Copyright © 2016 by Jay N. Forrest

All Rights Reserved. No part of this publication may be reproduced, stored in a retrieval system, or transmitted, in any form or in any means – by electronic, mechanical, photocopying, recording or otherwise – without prior written permission.

ISBN: 1519698755
ISBN-13: 978-1519698759

J.F. Books

Albuquerque, NM

www.JayForrest.org

DEDICATION

To

Stephen Batchelor
and
Ted Meissner

for being Trailblazers

CONTENTS

	Preface	9
1	My Struggle with Buddhism	11
2	Becoming a Secular Buddhist	15
3	Supernaturalism in Buddhism	19
4	Buddhism without Supernaturalism	25
5	Buddhism and Naturalism	31
6	Secular Buddhism	35
7	Buddhist But Not Religious	41
8	Buddhism Without Rebirth	43
9	Moment by Moment Re-Becoming	49
10	Rebirth and Science	55
11	Rebirth, Naturalism, and Evidence	63
12	No-Self and Rebirth	69
13	Psychological Karma	73
14	Psychological Samsara	75
15	Psychological Nirvana	79
16	Metaphysical Nirvana	83
17	There is no Buddhism without	85

Beliefs

Online Resources | 89
Bibliography | 91
About Author | 95

PREFACE

Chapter 6 was written exclusively for this book, otherwise the rest has appeared in some form before. Some have appeared as articles on my blog, well others are podcast episode transcripts. There inclusion here is because they all deal with the subject of secular Buddhism.

There will be some repetition, since theses were not originally designed for a book. There is also varying degrees of scholarship, since most of my writing is aimed at a popular readership.

I dedicated the book to Stephen Batchelor and Ted Meissner, both of much I have had the pleasure to interview. The opinions expressed in this book do not represent their views and any short comings are mine alone.

You will find in these pages that I sometimes refer to myself as a "secular Buddhist." I am completely comfortable being called a Humanist, but I am not altogether comfortable with the label "Buddhist."

But I am so profoundly influenced by the Dharma that it's hard not to be called some-kind-of-a-Buddhist. You could call me a secular Buddhist, the label does fits me. But as a self-designation, I am not altogether comfortable with it.

Maybe it is because, if I call myself a Buddhist, even a secular Buddhist, I am kind of obligated to follow the teachings of the Buddha. I am just not that devoted to the Buddha or his teachings. Rather, I am devoted to the truth and wisdom. But what is truth? The more I know, the less I know I know. Truth is relative and based on perspective and point of view.

So I practice nonattachment to views, even Buddhist ones. I could not say it better than Thich Nhat Hanh in this first two precepts of his *The Fourteen Precepts of Engaged Buddhism* (1987, 17). The first precept is, "Do not be idolatrous about or bound to any doctrine, theory, or ideology, even Buddhist ones. Buddhist systems of thought are guiding means; they are not absolute truth."

And the second precept is, "Do not think the knowledge you presently possess is changeless, absolute truth. Avoid being narrow minded and bound to present views. Learn and practice nonattachment from views in order to be open to receive others' viewpoints. Truth is found in life and not merely in conceptual knowledge. Be ready to learn throughout your entire life and to observe reality in yourself and in the world at all times."

If you don't already, I invite you to listen to and subscribe to my podcast. It is called The Jay Forrest Show and can be found at JayForrest.org. There you can also subscribe to my weekly newsletter and read my latest articles.

1

MY STRUGGLE WITH BUDDHISM

True rational consistency does not consist in stereotyping our opinions and views, and in refusing to make any improvement lest we should be guilty of change.

Rather, it consists in holding our minds open to receive the rays of truth from every direction. It consists in changing our views, language, and practice, as often and as fast, as we can obtain further information. I call this rational consistency, because this alone accords with a claim of being rational.

Claiming to be rational implies that one is honest and wants to know and obey all truth. It must follow, that rational consistency implies continued investigation and change of views and practice corresponding with increasing knowledge. No one should be afraid to change his views, his language, or his practices in conformity with increasing light.

The prevalence of such a fear would keep the world, at best, at a perpetual standstill, on all subjects of science, and consequently all improvements would be precluded. (Adapted from

Charles G. Finney, Systematic Theology.).

Rebirth

I want to explain why I almost gave up on Buddhism. There are hundreds of religions and philosophical systems, all of which claim to be the right one. How does one choose between them? For me, I want to believe only what I have evidence to believe. I am interested in living an evidence-based life. Traditional Buddhism has several issues that I have struggled with. The first issue I had was with rebirth or reincarnation. Where is the evidence? What reincarnates if there's no self? And if what is reborn is not me (the self), then why should I care?

Karma

The second issue I had was with Karma, which is understood to be the law of cause and effect. The evidence from science indicates that cause and effect are limited to this life. There's no evidence for an afterlife. Furthermore, the idea of cleansing or purifying bad Karma leads to the whole redemption and atonement mentality.

Superstition

The third issue I had was with the superstition you find in some forms of Buddhism. Seen more in later Mahayana Buddhism, such as psychic powers, ancestor worship, charms, spells, amulets, etc. You see this in Chinese Buddhism, where a statue of the Buddha is considered lucky. Stephen Batchelor tells the story of a Lama who tried to chase a storm away. Sorry, we can't control storms with our minds.

Superman
The fourth issue I had was with the belief that the Buddha was a superman of sorts. Saying he was "just a man" got me a flock of criticism on Reddit. I don't believe the Buddha was omniscient. That is an attribute for a god, not a man. No man has or ever will be all-knowing. Never happened, never will.

The Six Realms
The fifth issue I had was with the teaching of heavens and hells in Buddhism, as well as all the Six Realms. These are beliefs without scientific evidence. They may have psychological interpretations, but as metaphysical realities they are based on blind faith. Furthermore, I fail to understand how one can discover such things in meditation. Can one travel to Saturn in meditation and walk on its surface? Then why would we think that we can visit invisible realms in meditation?

Rituals and Customs
The sixth issue I had was with the rituals of Asian culture. Zen is a good example of this. Too many confuse the rituals and customs, with what Zen really is. Look at most Zen Centers and you will see that they copy their Asian ancestors. Tibetan Buddhism does the same. We need an American Buddhism that is integrated with American customs.

Vegetarianism
And the seventh and last issue I had was with Karmically enforced Vegetarianism. Buddhists are to never purposely kill an animal, or else we will get bad Karma. But what about our ancestors who

were hunter-gatherers, or Native Americans. As National Geographic Channel's show Life Below Zero illustrates, sometimes our survival depends on killing and eating meat. To say we are going to get a bad rebirth because of it, in my opinion, is silly. Furthermore, I don't believe that we are going to get bad Karma from killing a spider crawling in our bed, or exterminating the termites that are eating away at the foundations of our house.

For these reasons I dropped the "Buddhist" label for a while, as I tried to sort through things. I still believed in and practice mindfulness meditation. And I still respected certain aspects of Buddhism, such as mindfulness, wisdom, compassion, interdependence, impermanence, no-self, and that suffering originates in attachment.

Secular

I finally decided that there was just no better spiritual path for me than Buddhism. I decided that Secular Buddhism gave me all the Buddhism I needed, without the metaphysical baggage of prescientific India. This allows me to live an evidence-based life. Which, if you ask me, truly honors the Buddha's direction to "Be a lamp unto yourself" (SN 22.43).

Practical Buddhism, Chapter 110

2

BECOMING A SECULAR BUDDHIST

I want to share a little about my personal journey back to Buddhism. I also will introduce you to secular Buddhism as a legitimate form of modern Buddhism. And I will talk about being a Secular Buddhist.

My Personal Journey
First, I want to share a little of my personal journey that took place between September 2014, when I stopped doing the 5 Minute Dharma podcast, and August 2015, when I returned to doing it.

My struggles with Buddhism came to a head, when I realized that I simply could not believe in rebirth, metaphysical Karma, metaphysical Nirvana, the devas, heavens and hells, Hungry Ghosts, and morally obligated Vegetarianism.

There is simply no evidence for these things, and any supposed evidence for such things is questionable at best. In fact, it is not better, or different, from the many claims made by other religions. Although I knew that the Buddha tended to shun metaphysical questions, traditional Buddhism has not.

In a conversation on Reddit, I was told that my beliefs were not in line with Buddhism and that I was not a "Buddhist." Even now I still get this kind of feedback. One of the commenters on my website said, "you can't be a Buddhist without believing in the possibility of rebirth."

But back then, such comments made me think, "If I wasn't a Buddhist, what was I?" It was then that I began a long and detailed search through the worldview catalog, and discovered four traditions that offered a spirituality without God or supernaturalism.

I first explored Humanism and was impressed, but it lacked a developed spirituality. I then explored Scientific Pantheism and agreed that the world is sacred, but the idea of the universe being God didn't sit right with me. I finally explored Religious or Spiritual Naturalism and found that it was primarily an ethic based on ecological concerns.

I still consider myself a Spiritual Naturalist, but I view it more as an umbrella term, that includes any spirituality without God or the supernatural. The only problem with Spiritual Naturalism is that it lacks its own spirituality, rather it tends to borrow practices from other spiritual traditions, including Buddhism. Which led me back to Buddhism as the anchor for practice. Buddhism has a depth of wisdom which no other tradition can match.

Secular Buddhism

Second, I rediscovered a scientifically legitimate form of Buddhism. Secular Buddhism is not a religion, but a spiritual path centered in practice. It is skeptical of any teachings that are not supported by scientific or psychological evidence.

There is no scientific proof of rebirth. There are rational explanations, but they all rest on unprovable assumptions. Hence, Secular Buddhists don't believe in a literal rebirth after death, or the supernatural for that matter. They tend to view the Sutras as a mix of tradition and authentic teachings of the Buddha, and should be studied critically.

The problem was, is it right to call yourself a "Buddhist" if you reject some traditional teachings of Buddhism? At first, I didn't think that it was, and many would agree. But I have changed my mind.

Stephen Batchelor's book, *Confessions of a Buddhist Atheist*, helped me to rethink the issue. Another book that helped me along was *Waking Up* by well-known atheist Sam Harris. He showed me that one can be skeptical and still practice Buddhist meditation and follow Buddhist principles.

The last book that influenced me was the Dalai Lama's, *Beyond Religion*, where he endorses secular ethics. In it he says, "I believe the time has come to find a way of thinking about spirituality and ethics that is beyond religion."

Secular Buddhism is one way to think about Buddhist spirituality beyond the confines of the traditional Buddhist religion. I finally came to the conclusion that it is appropriate to call yourself a Buddhist, that is, if you qualify it with the adjective "secular."

I believe that the Buddha Dharma is evolving and adapting itself to modern secular culture. The new emerging face of the Dharma is secular Buddhism, the fourth vehicle of Buddhism.

Fascination with Labels

Third, so what am I then? We are fascinated with labels, aren't we? We see people through labels, and many times never meet the person on the other side. I believe secular Buddhism is the best spiritual path out there for the modern world. It is all the Buddhism you need for practice, without the metaphysical baggage.

If you need a label, you can call me a Secular Buddhist. I am committed to the foundational teachings of the Buddha, such as the Four Noble Truths, the Eightfold Noble Path, and Three Marks of Existence.

In the podcast, I try to focus on the teachings and practices that lead to freedom from attachment, aversion, and delusion. I also share the latest findings of psychology and neuroscience. I hope the podcast will help people live an intelligent and enlightened life of inner freedom and happiness.

I have shared a little about my personal journey back to Buddhism. I introduced you to secular Buddhism as a legitimate and modern form of Buddhism. And I talked about being a Secular Buddhist.

August 7, 2015, Podcast

3

SUPERNATURALISM IN BUDDHISM

Buddhism began in the age of myth and magic, in a world that believed in an invisible supernatural realm that were filled with gods, angels, demons, and ghosts. In this age, miracles were common and shamans did extraordinary signs and wonders. It was a time where the mind was given to superstition and magical thinking.

Buddhism was not immune to this. It is reported in The Middle Length Discourses of the Buddha, that the future Buddha, "passed away from the Tusita heaven and descended into his mother's womb" (MN 123). When he descended, "four young deities came to guard him at the four quarters so that no human or non-human or anyone at all could harm the Bodhisatta or his mother" (NM 123).

Buddha's Virgin Birth

The tradition teaches that the Buddha, whose name was Siddhartha Gautama, had a virgin birth. The story goes that Siddhartha's mother had a dream of a white elephant, holding a white lotus flower in its trunk. It appeared and went round her three times. It then entered her womb through her right side, and she became pregnant. The king, Siddhartha's father, asked the wise men about the dream. They told him, "Your Majesty, you are very lucky. The devas [gods] have chosen our queen as the mother of the Purest-One and the child will become a very great being" (Life of the Buddha 2002, 8).

But the miracles didn't stop at his conception, they continued in his birth. The Buddha to be was not born like normal babies. He did not come out of the vaginal canal, but "he came out of his mother's side" (Conze 1959, 35). And immediately after being born, he stood up, took seven steps, and declared, "For enlightenment I was born, for the good of all that lives. This is the last time that I have been born into the world of becoming" (Conze 1959, 36). It says that every place the baby Buddha placed his foot, a lotus flower bloomed (Life of the Buddha 2002, 9). The Middle Length Discourses of the Buddha says, "When the Bodhisatta came forth from his mother's womb, first gods received him, then human beings" (NM 123).

Now all this talk about a virgin birth, talking newborns, and gods may make some people uncomfortable. Others will toss it aside as not reflecting the earliest Buddhist scriptures, known as the Pali text.

Yet many of the texts I just quoted were from the Pali Canon. Now it is true that many of the legends of the Buddha's birth did arise after the Pali text, but many are found in it as well. And more importantly, many of these myths are still believed and taught by many traditional Buddhists today.

Modern Buddhist Teachers

For example, Geshe Kelsang Gyatso (1993, 3), in his book *Introduction to Buddhism*, not only teaches this very story but explains that, when the Buddha was born, "Brahma and Indra took the child painlessly from her side." So many traditional Buddhists believe that the Buddha was born of a virgin, and had a miraculous and painless birth.

But the miracles don't stop at Siddhartha's birth. "As the young prince grew up," explains Geshe Kelsang Gyatso (1993, 4), "he mastered all the traditional arts and sciences without needing any instruction. He knew sixty-four different languages, each with their own alphabet, and he was also very skilled at mathematics."

In the Pali Canon

And yes, the miracles of the Buddha can be found in the Pali Canon. As Vessantara (2004, 183) explains, "In the Mahayana sutras and in the Pali Canon psychic powers, including clairvoyance, clairaudience, telepathy, levitation, and memory of past lives, are frequently mentioned." N. K. G. Mendis (2006) explains that "The Buddhist texts recognize five laws holding sway over the natural order." The fourth one is, the "Law of the mind (cittaniyaama) [which] governs the order of consciousness and mental processes and also makes possible such feats as telepathy, telekinesis, clairvoyance, clairaudience, and recollection of past lives."

Here is one of the Suttas of what the Buddha reportedly said about the superpowers of monks:

"a bhikkhu wields the various kinds of spiritual power: having been one, he becomes many;

having been many, he becomes one; he appears and vanishes; he goes unhindered through a wall, through a rampart, through a mountain as though through space; he dives in and out of the earth as though it were water; he walks on water without sinking as though it were earth; seated cross-legged, he travels in space like a bird; with his hands he touches and strokes the moon and sun so powerful and mighty; he exercises mastery with the body as far as the brahma world" (SN 51.11).

Or you can read about the thirty-two marks of a Great Man. In the Lakkana Sutta, it says that the Buddha, being a Great Man, has these thirty-two marks. One of the marks is that "his male organs are enclosed in a sheath" (DN 30). Or we can read about how Sakka, "lord of the gods," decided to consult the Buddha (DN 21). And there are many other examples.

Modernized Buddhism

You usually don't hear about this side of Buddhism. As David McMahan (2008, 5) explains, "What many Americans and Europeans often understand by the term 'Buddhism,' however, is actually a modern hybrid tradition with roots in the European Enlightenment no less than the Buddha's enlightenment, in Romanticism and transcendentalism as much as the Pali canon, and in the clash of Asian cultures and colonial powers as much as in mindfulness and meditation."

By what principle have contemporary Buddhist teachers used to adapt ancient Buddhism to the modern world? The clearest statement is by the Dalai Lama (2005, 3), "if scientific analysis were conclusively to demonstrate certain claims in Buddhism to be false, then we must accept the findings of science and abandon those claims."

Notice where the Dalai Lama places the burden of proof. Buddhism doesn't have to produce evidence for its claims, rather science has to "conclusively" demonstrate a claim in Buddhism to be false. This is all backward.

The Burden of Proof

A person who makes a claim that asserts something is so, has the burden to support it with evidence. In other words, if you are saying something is so, it is your obligation to prove it. The skeptic is under no obligation to accept a mere assertion. Furthermore, the skeptic who denies the claim has no obligation to prove a negative. In many cases, it is impossible to prove a negative. All the skeptic has to do is disprove the evidence for the purported claim.

By shifting the burden of proof, the Dalai Lama can continue to believe and teach reincarnation. How can you "conclusively" demonstrate that the reincarnation claim is false? It is like Carl Sagan's invisible dragon in his garage. Buddhists can "counter every physical test you propose with a special explanation of why it won't work" (Sagan 1996, 171).

If I made the claim that there is a teapot buried on the dwarf planet Pluto, you would likely not believe me. But you could not "conclusively" demonstrate that the claim is false, either. To say that you have to believe me until you can prove me wrong is ridiculous. But this is exactly what traditional Buddhists ask of the skeptic.

The simple fact is, in the words of Carl Sagan

(1996, 171), "Claims that cannot be tested, assertions immune to disproof are veridically worthless, whatever value they may have in inspiring us or in exciting our sense of wonder."

March 7, 2016, Blog

4

BUDDHISM WITHOUT SUPERNATURALISM

"Do not be led by reports, or tradition, or hearsay. Be not led by the authority of religious texts, nor by mere logic or inference, nor by considering appearances, nor by the delight in speculative opinions, nor by seeming possibilities, nor by the idea: 'this is our teacher.'" (Kalama Sutta [Rahula 1974, 2-3]).

The Question

So the question is, Owen Flanagan (2011, xi) asks, "Is it possible to take an ancient comprehensive philosophy like Buddhism, subtract the hocus pocus, and have a worthwhile philosophy for twenty-first-century scientifically informed secular thinkers?" Secular Buddhists believe that it is possible.

Reinterpreting Buddhism

But you might wonder, by what right do secular Buddhists have in redefining and reinterpreting Buddhism? Surely you can't be a Buddhist without accepting a literal rebirth? Buddhism, as John Snelling (1998, Caveat) rightly points out, "is not an authoritarian religion with a centralized authority that grants or with-holds the seal of approval. It is therefore up to the individual to test the ground for him- or herself."

This is, in fact, what the Buddha encouraged in the Kalama Sutta, "Be not led by the authority of religious texts." Just because you find something in the Buddhist scriptures, doesn't mean that it is true or that you have to believe it. You should think it through, evaluate the evidence, look at the pragmatic results of it, and choose accordingly.

The Poisoned Arrow

This is what is confusing to many Buddhist who study the Suttas. At times, you have clear superstitious and supernatural statements, and then you have rational statements like the Kalama Sutta.

Other examples include the Sutta on the parable of the Poisoned Arrow. It tells about a man who was wounded by a poisoned arrow. They took him to the doctor, but he refused treatment until he knew who shot the arrow, his status, clan, height, skin color, where he lives, what kind of bow he used, and many similar questions.

The Buddha said:

"All this would still not be known to that man and meanwhile he would die. So too, Malunkyaputta, if anyone should say thus: 'I will not lead the holy life under the Blessed One until the Blessed One declares to me: 'the world is eternal' and 'the world is not eternal'; 'the world is finite' and 'the world is infinite'; 'the soul is the same as the body' and 'the soul is one thing and the body another'; and 'after death a Tathagata exists' and 'after death a Tathagata does not exist' and 'after death a Tathagata both exists and does not exist' and 'after death a Tathagata neither exists nor does not exist,' that would still remain undeclared by the Tathagata and meanwhile that person would die" (MN 63).

Here we see that the Buddha tended to shun metaphysical questions and was basically a pragmatist. As Thich Nhat Hanh (1995, 42) points out, "The Buddha always told his disciples not to waste their time and energy in metaphysical speculation." Later Buddhist couldn't resist these questions. This is demonstrated by such writers as Nagarjuna, Vasubandhu, Santaraksita, Mipam Namgyel, Dogan, and Nishitani (Edelglass and Garfield 2009, 9-12).

Simile of the Raft

Another example of the rational and pragmatic side of the Buddhist presentation of the Buddha is the Simile of the Raft. In it the Buddha says that the Dharma "is similar to a raft, being for the purpose of crossing over, not for the purpose of grasping." Once you use the raft to cross from one shore of a river to the other, you abandon the raft. So, the Buddha concludes, "when you know the Dhamma to be similar to a raft, you should abandon even the teachings, how much more so things contrary to the teachings" (NM 22).

Yet, we see traditional Buddhist attached to the teaching of cosmic karma and rebirth. They refuse to "abandon even the teachings" that are clearly unscientific. They cannot honestly look at the evidence and follow it to where it leads.

And worse than that, some cannot help but attack those who have laid down the raft. I have been repeatedly told that I cannot be a Buddhist if I don't believe in rebirth. They need to hear the wise words of Thich Nhat Hanh (1993, 17). The first of the Fourteen Guidelines for Engaged Buddhism states, "Do not be idolatrous about or bound to any doctrine, theory, or ideology, even Buddhist ones. Buddhist systems of thought are guiding means; they are not absolute truth."

Attachment to Views

The Buddha encouraged his disciples to not be attached to views. "Why is it, Master Kaccana, that ascetics fight with ascetics? It is, brahmin, because of attachment to views, adherence to views, fixation on views, addiction to views, obsession with views, holding firmly to views that ascetics fight with ascetics" (AN 2.37). Clearly being attached to views is not a good thing. Yet many Buddhist are.

All these passages show that the picture of the Buddha in the Pali Canon is mixed with many different voices. How many of these voices go back to the historical Buddha, we simply don't know. We have to remember that the Pali Canon was an oral tradition passed down from one generation to another for over 500 years. Corruption, exaggeration, and embellishment was not only likely, but certain.

So, as David McMahan (2008, 5) explains, "The popular picture of Buddhism is neither unambiguously 'there' in the ancient texts and lived traditions nor merely a fantasy of an educated elite population in the West, an image with no corresponding object." It is because the earliest texts have this strange mix that modern interpreters can pick and choose that which speaks to the current culture.

Superstitious Monks

But it is also possible, that the voice of the historical Buddha was drowned out and distorted by generations of superstitious monks. As Stephen Batchelor (2015, 3) explained, "Although the Buddha may have presented his ideas in the context of multiple lifetimes, this often-repeated passage implies that he did so for cultural and pragmatic reasons alone." He then quotes the Kalama Sutta, "'Of that which the wise (pundita) in the world agree upon as not existing,' he said, 'I too say that it does not exist. And of that which the wise in the world agree upon as existing, I too say that it exists'" (Batchelor 2015, 3).

Could it be that the Buddha was just a product of his time? As Stephen T. Asma (2011, 149) points out, "There is nothing particularly Buddhist about either of these metaphysical doctrines – karma and rebirth…. They are leftovers from pre-Buddhist religion and found their way onto the Buddhist plate for cultural, not philosophical, reasons."

The real foundation of science is naturalism. Naturalism is, according to *Webster's New World Dictionary*, the view that "the natural world, known and experienced scientifically, is all that exists and that there is no supernatural or spiritual creation, control, or significance." So secular Buddhism is another way of referring to a Buddhism the follows or is based upon naturalistic principles.

March 9, 2016, Blog

5

BUDDHISM AND NATURALISM

Traditional Buddhism began over 2,500 years ago. It was founded on the metaphysical understandings of the time. In this age of myth and magic, all the world was supernatural. There were invisible beings and mystical realms everywhere.

For ancient civilization, there was no such thing as naturalism. They had no way to distinguish, let alone conceive, of a difference between the natural world and the supernatural.

Cutting Through the Vale
The first to begin to cut through the vale were the Greeks. They began looking for natural explanations rather than supernatural ones. This is the first time in recorded history where someone was using methodological naturalism in the investigation of nature. But their writing were lost during the dark ages.

The European Renaissance
Their rediscovery gave birth the European

Renaissance of the 14th century. According to the *Online Etymology Dictionary*, naturalism was first used "as a view of the world and humanity's relationship to it" in 1750.

Why is this date important, because it was in the middle of the 18th century. It was at the height of the Enlightenment, which resulted in the French and American revolutions. It set the stage for the emergence of modern science during the 19th century.

Buddha Studied the Mind

Buddhism was started by Siddhartha Gautama in India, somewhere around the 5th century BCE. It should be expected that he would view the world very much like others of his age. His great subject of study was not the world, but the human mind. His one great quest was to discover the cause and cure for the mental and emotional pain and discomfort of human life.

It should come as no surprise that the Buddha did not question the basic worldview he grew up in. Science was still thousands of years away. What is surprising is just how accurate he was about the psychological nature of human beings. Neuroscience and psychology are verifying the Buddha's observations and confirming the benefits of meditation and mindfulness.

Metaphysical Baggage

But many scientifically minded students of Buddhism have run up against the metaphysical baggage of the Buddha's teachings. They have read about the six realms, devas, heavens, hells, karma, and reincarnation. These are the leftovers from a prescientific worldview. They are the supernaturalism of ancient India.

Naturalistic Buddhism

So the question is, can we replace the supernaturalism of ancient India with the naturalism of modern science? I believe we can, and here is why. The Buddha never made the metaphysical elements foundational to his teachings. His teachings stand whether or not we believe in rebirth, the six realms, or any other of the unprovable speculations. The reason is, because he based his teachings on the reality of suffering, the cause of suffering, and the cure for suffering.

In other words, the Buddha wisely founded his teachings on empirically verifiable experience. The great insights that have arisen from his teachings and directions are continually being verified by the mind sciences. Meditation works without beliefs. Mindfulness works without metaphysical beliefs. The Buddha taught us not what to think, but how to practice. He taught us how to see reality for ourselves, and not take his word for it. After all, second hand knowledge never set anyone free.

New and Improved Buddhism

So we can and should replace the supernaturalism of ancient India with the naturalism of modern science. The resulting product would not be traditional Buddhism, but it would be a new and improved Buddhism – secular Buddhism. What you call it is really not important, what matters is that we use the practices of the Buddha and the insights of neuroscience to improve our lives and the lives of our children.

October 5, 2015, Blog

6

SECULAR BUDDHISM

Secular Buddhism has had a brief history. In a search of Google Scholar, I found a few mentions of "secular Buddhism" from the 80's. The first goes back to 1983. In this instance, David L. Gosling makes a passing reference to "Chiang Mai's 'Secular' Buddhism."

Then in 1998, we have Hyun-key Kim Hogarth use the term in a paper entitled, "Rationality, practicality and Modernity: Buddhism, Shamanism and Christianity in Contemporary Korean Society." In the article he says, "From the sociological, particularly functionalist, point of view, then the forms of secular Buddhism practiced in Southeast Asia, though they involve theological 'heresy', can be regarded as the successful transformation of essentially unsociable Buddhism into a social religion."

Now both of these reference do not refer to secular Buddhism as we understand it today. But they do illustrate an awareness of the growing use of *secular* to refer to aspects of Buddhism that are less religious. I think both references carry this connotation.

In Britain, the first use of "secular Buddhism" in Google Scholar is by Jeremy Holmes in 2000. In his article, "NHS Psychotherapy - Past, Future and Present," he writes, "I will start with a credo, one which tries to balance psychodynamics with a kind of secular Buddhism which, I believe, is compatible with the values of psychotherapy." This is clearly speaking of "secular Buddhism" as we now mean it.

The Beginnings of Secular Buddhism

Since David L. McMahan (2008, 8) has already done the work, I will simply summarize him here. The modernization of buddhism began with Soen Shaku, Dwight Godard, and D. T. Suzuki, and progressed through the efforts of the Dalai Lama, Alan Watts, Thich Nhat Hanh, Shunryu Suzuki, and many others.

The problem is that people were not told that this Buddhism was a modernized version, but where led to believe that it was Buddhism in its purer more original form. Which may or may not be true, depending upon your interpretation.

A better approach and a more open one, is to be forthright about the desire to adapt the teachings of the Buddha to the naturalistic and secular viewpoint of the West. And this is exactly what Stephen Batchelor has done.

Stephen Batchelor, and my friend Ted Meissner, are perhaps the best known popularizers of secular Buddhism today. Stephen Batchelor is a contemporary Buddhist teacher and writer, best known for his secular or agnostic approach to Buddhism. Stephen considers Buddhism to be a constantly evolving culture of awakening rather than a religious system based on immutable dogmas and beliefs. His latest book is *After*

Buddhism: Rethinking the Dharma for a Secular Age.

Ted Meissner is the Executive Director of the Secular Buddhist Association and the podcast host of the Secular Buddhist. The Secular Buddhist Association has been a gathering place for those with secular views.

What is Secular Buddhism?

Stephen Batchelor (2015, 231) defines a secular Buddhist as "one who is committed to the practice of the dharma for the sake of this world alone." So a secular approach to Buddhism, explains Stephen Batchelor (2015, 16), "is thus concerned with how the dharma can enable humans and other living beings to flourish in this biosphere, not in a hypothetical afterlife.

Mark W. Gura (2015, 218) defines secular Buddhism as the "Theory and practice of Buddhism that makes no supernatural claims and advocates only those elements that are consistent with or corroborated by reason and the best science available."

Rick Bateman (2010) defines it this way, "Secular Buddhism is a non-religious form of Buddhism unique to the West. Tradition, robes and ritual are absent as are non-English terms. It is devoid of authority through title or lineage. It is atheistic i.e. there is no consideration of the supernatural or reincarnation. Karma is considered only in the sense the word as commonly used in English – of one's intentions, actions and their results in this life."

Here is Noah Rasheta's (2016) definition, "Secular Buddhism is a modern approach to understanding the deep wisdom contained with

Buddhist philosophy but without any of the superstitious and supernatural beliefs that can't be observed/tested through empirical research. Secular Buddhism is based on humanist, skeptical, and/or agnostic values as well as pragmatism, rather than religious beliefs. It treats Buddhism as an applied philosophy, rather than a religion."

From this, we can see that secular Buddhism is a broad term for an emerging form of Buddhism that approaches the supernatural or paranormal claims of Buddhism with a skeptical or agnostic attitude.

Original Buddhism

In its original form, writes A. C. Grayling (2013, 16), Buddhism "is a philosophy, not a religion." Buddhism began as a nontheistic philosophy and way of life based on the teachings of Siddhartha Gautama, who is commonly known as the Buddha.

This is why many secular Buddhists search the Pali canon to discern more closely what originated with Gautama, and what was added later. Textual criticism is still in its easy stages within Buddhism.

Buddhism as Philosophy

Secular Buddhism is an adaption of the philosophy of the Buddha to a naturalistic worldview. It is Buddhism without metaphysical beliefs. Take Buddhism, minus the supernatural elements, and you have a secular Buddhism.

Now how it all plays out in actual practice differs between thinkers. Most take an agnostic view towards such things as karma, rebirth, psychic abilities, and other such metaphysical claims.

A Spiritual Path

Secular Buddhism is not a religion, but a spiritual path centered in practice. It is skeptical of any teachings that are not supported by scientific and psychological evidence.

There is no scientific proof of rebirth. There are rational explanations, but they all rest on unprovable assumptions. Hence, Secular Buddhists don't believe in a literal rebirth after death or the supernatural (such as heavens and hells). It views the Sutras as a mix of tradition and authentic teachings of the Buddha, and should be studied critically.

Secular Buddhism is one way to think about Buddhist spirituality beyond the confines of traditional Buddhist religion. I finally came to the conclusion, that it is appropriate to call myself a Buddhist, if I qualify it with the adjective "secular."

I believe that the Buddha Dharma is evolving and adapting itself to modern secular culture. The new emerging face of the Dharma is secular Buddhism, the fourth vehicle of Buddhism.

Deconstructing Buddhism

The problem most secular Buddhists struggle with is how to adapt Buddhism to the modern world. At one level, you can remove the supernatural from Buddhism and place it on a naturalistic foundation.

This process will mean rehumanizing the Buddha, naturalizing rebirth, naturalizing Karma, naturalizing Nirvana, naturalizing the Six Realms, clarifying the Four Noble Truths and the Eightfold Noble Path, and democratizing the Sangha.

Humanism and Buddhism

I find myself drawn to both Humanism, for its

naturalistic and rationalistic viewpoint, and Buddhism, for its practical approaches to personal fulfillment.

For me, Humanism is great for critical inquiry and social concern, but not so strong on personal fulfillment. Humanism will never be a widespread movement until it addresses what religious people call "spirituality."

But what if we converged Humanism and Buddhism? What would the result look like. I don't know, but I have some ideas.

Zen Humanism

So what do you call a secularized Dharma? Some call it secular Buddhism. But that has connotations that some secular Humanists don't like. So what about Zen Humanism?

Zen is already a word that is associated with meditation. So it has advantages there. Meditation is scientifically shown to improve people's lives.

Groping for an Answer

In my 2016 interview with Stephen Batchelor, we talked about the future of Buddhism and a wider practice. I think he is right, we are groping for something that our language is not yet able to handle. Secular spirituality is a term as problematic as naturalistic spirituality.

So here I am, on the very tip of a wave. I am trying to name it, identify it, and help give it shape. But I feel like I am groping in the dark. I struggle to give it words, but I feel it.

It is coming.

7

BUDDHIST BUT NOT RELIGIOUS

Is Buddhism a religion? It depends on your definition of religion.

Ask a bunch of Buddhist teachers and you will get a bunch of different answers.

The real question is, what is religion? You have to answer that before you can answer whether or not Buddhism is a religion.

What is a Religion?

Philosopher Daniel Dennett's working definition of religion is, "social systems whose participants avow belief in a supernatural agent or agents whose approval is to be sought."

Clearly Buddhism is not a religion according to this definition.

What if we turn to the English Dictionary? Merriam-Webster.com gives the first definition of religion as, "the belief in a god or in a group of gods." The second definition is, "an organized system of beliefs, ceremonies, and rules used to worship a god or a group of gods."

Again, Buddhism is not a religion according to this definition.

The third definition of religion in Merriam-Webster.com is, "an interest, a belief, or an activity that is very important to a person or group." Clearly Buddhism is a religion according to this definition, but so is sports and sex.

Buddhism is a Spirituality

I contend that Buddhism is a spirituality and not a religion.

Spirituality is a way of valuing that is most comprehensively and intensively experienced (cf. Frederick Ferre). Religion is about beliefs, spirituality is about experience.

Buddhism is a spiritual philosophy designed to foster a way of life that leads to seeing reality as it is and results in being free from suffering and dissatisfaction.

September 21, 2015, Blog

8

BUDDHISM WITHOUT REBIRTH

You can be a Buddhist without believing in reincarnation or rebirth. You don't have to kiss your brains goodbye when you become a Buddhist. You don't have to buy into a 2,500 year old cosmology which included heavens, hells, and a host of mythological places and beings.

To paraphrase the Buddha from the Kalama Sutta:

> Do not believe in anything simply because you have heard it; Do not simply believe in traditions, because they have been handed down for many generations; Do not simply believe in anything, because it is spoken and rumored by many; Do not believe in anything simply because it is found written in your religious books; But after observation and analysis, when you find that anything agrees with reason and is conducive to the good and benefit of one and all, then accept it and live up to it" (Guruge and Amaradasa 1956, 39).

Let's do this with the teaching of rebirth.

No Evidence

First, there is no evidence for rebirth. Science tells us what exists, spirituality tells us what it means. Science deals with objective facts, Buddhism deals with subjective experiences.

Science has, in fact, studied reincarnation and can get no better evidence than anecdotal testimonials. That is, personal stories that cannot be scientifically verified and are no better than other religions' stories of visits of angels, Jesus, or demons. They have the evidential weight of an infomercial, where person after person tells you how great their product is.

Science has reached the conclusion, based on "observation and analysis," to use the Buddha's words, that consciousness does not exist outside of a brain. As Sue Blackmore (2008) points out in an article in *The Guardian*, "If human consciousness can really leave the body and operate without a brain then everything we know in neuroscience has to be questioned." This is why I don't believe in a literal rebirth. There is no evidence that consciousness survives the death of the brain.

I am not a materialist, I am an evidentialist. I am dedicated to a method, not a conclusion. The Buddha told us to believe something only after careful observation and analysis. Only when it agrees with reason and is conducive to the good and benefit of all, should we accept it.

Rebirth does not agree with reason or scientific observation. Furthermore, I find that many modern Buddhists simply don't care about rebirth. It is either meaningless or irrelevant.

The Buddha Taught It

Second, there is little question that the Buddha taught rebirth. It seems quit clear that, if the Suttas are to be believed, that the Buddha believed and taught rebirth. It was a common teaching in ancient India at the time.

Now whether he ever questioned the reality of rebirth, we don't know. It is possible that he had some kind of spiritual experience that convinced him of it. But it is also possible that he was just being pragmatic, worrying more about spiritual practice than metaphysical questions.

In this case, maybe rebirth should be seen as a skillful means used by the Buddha to motivate ethics and Dharma practice. The Buddha may have been just as skeptical as you and me, but found it ingrained in his students minds. So he, therefore, used it as a motivation for ethics and self-discipline. Rebirth could have been just a skillful means, a pragmatic tool. We will probably never know the answer.

But either way, with our current science, we find no evidence for the reality of rebirth or reincarnation. So is the belief in rebirth wrong? I don't know, since we cannot disprove rebirth, any more than we can disprove a Creator God. But, as I say in my book *Humanism, God, and the Bible*, "A person who makes a claim that asserts something is so, has the burden to support it with evidence."

The reason I question whether the Buddha really believed in any kind of literal reincarnation, is that he so modified it, that the resulting doctrine required a new name. It is called "rebirth" instead of "reincarnation," and most traditional Buddhists still distinguish the two.

This was because the Buddha taught that there is no-self; that self or ego was just an illusion. But the no-self teaching removes the agent from rebirth. So what is reborn, if "you" are an illusion? See how the transference of the inner you to another body is impossible. There is no inner you in Buddhism.

Reincarnation makes no sense in a Buddhist context. And theories trying to explain Buddhist rebirth fills volumes. But some traditional Buddhists are willing to divide the Sangha over this. Some even bar teachers who do not believe this rebirth dogma from teaching at their places.

The Living Dharma

Third, Dharma, if it is alive, will change, adapt, and evolve. When something is dead it stops changing, stops growing. It no longer adapts to the world as it unfolds.

The vitality of Buddhism can be seen in its adaptability to modernity. The fact that Buddhism is evolving and growing in the West is a sign that it is alive.

But not everybody is happy about the new face of the Dharma. Some traditional Buddhists do not like the way the Dharma is growing in the West. They would like to control it, moderate it, but they cannot.

The new Dharma is not enough like the old Dharma for them, therefore they call it a "rupture." Supposedly, we secular Buddhists are not taking the Buddha's teachings serious enough. They tell us that we cannot have Buddhism without rebirth.

Since it's not their Buddhism, it doesn't qualify as Buddhism. Since they are attached to their views of what the Dharma is, they can't conceive of it in any other way. They do not understand, though they should, that their attachment to views is causing their discomfort over secular Buddhism.

The Dharma is a living thing, therefore it will adapt and evolve in the new soil of the secular West. It should not come as a surprise that people invested in the old Dharma, may not like the new Dharma. But which would we like, wildlife or no life. Set the Dharma free.

August 14, 2015, Podcast

9

MOMENT BY MOMENT RE-BECOMING

The Buddha himself encouraged us, in the Kalama Sutta, to only accept a teaching "when you yourselves know" it is true (AN 3.65). Rebirth or reincarnation is a teaching without scientific evidence. There are rational explanations, but they all rest on unprovable assumptions. The Buddha's teachings have authority only in so far as the evidence validates them. I am committed to evidence, not tradition. I think the Buddha would approve, for I am being a "refuge" unto myself (DN 16).

An Agnostic Approach

First, there is the agnostic approach to rebirth. The fact is, that the Buddha taught rebirth (cf. MN 39). But with our current science, we find no evidence for the reality of rebirth or reincarnation. But likewise, we cannot disprove rebirth. It might be true.

So some practitioners take an agnostic view of rebirth and just say, "I don't know, maybe." This is common among Zen and Insight Meditation teachers. I used to take this view myself, until I began getting deeper into the study of neuroscience. Now I believe that the evidence is actually against it.

A samurai once asked Zen Master Hakuin where he would go after he died. Hakuin answered, "How am I supposed to know?" "How do you not know? You're a Zen Master!" exclaimed the samurai. "Yes, but not a dead one," Hakuin answered. For Zen, literal rebirth is not an essential teaching.

It seems clear that Zen Master Dogen did not believe in a literal rebirth. He said, "Firewood, after becoming ash, does not again become firewood. Similarly, human beings, after death, do not live again." The same is true for Secular Buddhists.

Psychological Reinterpretation

Second, we can reinterpret rebirth psychologically. Literal rebirth is a teaching without scientific evidence. But before we throw the baby out with the bathwater, is there a nugget of truth here?

The Pali word *punabbhava* is usually translated as "rebirth." However, it literally means "re-becoming." Can we keep the concept of repeated becoming, if we limit it to this one life? I think we can, let me explain.

A number of meditation teachers have taught that we can look at rebirth in the light of the mind remaking itself moment to moment. Reginald Ray explains that, "Each arising of consciousness is conditioned by the previous arising and in turn sets up conditions for subsequent arising."

Everything is impermanent, our minds are

changing moment by moment. What gets reborn or repeated in the next moment, is what was planted by the previous moment. We reinvent ourselves every day by the seeds we planted the day before.

In this sense, Karma is the planting of seeds that will bloom in the future. The Karma within this one life, which is intentional thought or deeds, will affect us for good or ill. How we live now, influences how we will be tomorrow. What we sow in this life, we reap in this life. It is limited to this one life.

I think that moment to moment re-becoming is an important application of the Buddha's teaching. It is taking what the Buddha said about rebirth seriously, but applying it to the present moment. It also avoids unnecessary metaphysical speculations.

This understand can be the key to developing ourselves into the people we want to be. It is by intentionally changing our thoughts and actions in the present moment, that we become better, wiser, and happier. As the saying goes, "Sow a thought, reap an action; sow an action, reap a habit; sow a habit, reap a character."

Every day we are either re-becoming what we were, or we can become something better, wiser, and plant the seeds of a happy tomorrow. This moment to moment re-becoming is a rebirth we can believe in, and we can experience it every day of our lives.

Our Legacy

Third, we can see a sort of re-becoming in our actions. There is a rebirth, of sorts, in the effect of our actions in the lives of others. In fact, there is an endless chain of causes and effects. Our lives influence people for good or evil. We leave a lasting influence upon the people we meet, and the places we have been.

What will be the legacy we leave behind for coming generations? As we destroy the environment, increase the gap between the rich and poor, and lose intimacy with one another. What are we leaving behind? This collective Karma will re-become in the future generations of humankind.

If we take self out of the equation, we can think of humanity as being reborn with every new child that comes into the world. Here our past actions have a direct and immediate effect on the future of humankind. This is a rebirth that will determine the survival of the human species. We are re-birthing habits and attitudes that will one day be our downfall.

The evidence for a personal rebirth is lacking, at best. But the concept of re-becoming can be applied to moment by moment choices within this one life.

And one last way we can reinterpret re-becoming is applying it to matter and energy. Our DNA is passed from one generation to the next. This may be what the Buddha actually sensed, but didn't have the words for. This is a way, the only way, that I can and will continue after death. My DNA, which is a part of who I am, will continue in my son and daughters. They, in turn, will pass it on to their children. So in this sense I continue, but without a self.

In conclusion, I have suggested a number of ways to reinterpret rebirth. All of these eliminate the metaphysical speculation and are scientifically justifiable. Taking rebirth as a metaphor, re-becoming can inform and inspire Right Action, Right Speech, and Right Effort.

August 21, 2015, Podcast

10

REBIRTH AND SCIENCE

Whenever I write that "there is no evidence for rebirth," I sometimes will get someone who will respond that, "Yes, there is."

What they are talking about is testimonies of people, who have supposedly been reincarnated, and can remember their past life. This is not "evidence" in any meaningful sense.

For evidence to count it has to be verifiable and subject to falsification. If a claim is made that is above and beyond falsification, then it is not evidence (Popper). It is not evidence simply because it is beyond verification.

Best Kind of Evidence

Our best kind of evidence is scientific evidence. "Scientific evidence is evidence which serves to either support or counter a scientific theory or hypothesis. Such evidence is expected to be empirical evidence and interpretation in accordance with scientific method" (Wikipedia).

Give me scientific evidence, not mere assertion. A person may have faith that rebirth is true, but they do not have scientific evidence.

Discrediting Science

The next thing a person will sometimes do is to discredit science. Since science does not support their pet theory, they invent reasons not to trust science. Science asks the world questions in the form of experiments, and the results of these experiments are nature's answers. If you don't like the answers, talk to nature, not science.

Science gives us the only reliable knowledge of what exists. Religion is not a better way to arrive at the truth of what exists. No two religions can agree on what actually exists metaphysically. Who is to say that Buddhism got their metaphysics right?

Yes, science has its limitations. But its reach and accuracy far exceed that of any other branch of human knowledge, this includes religion, philosophy, and mystical experiences.

Limitations of Introspection

The mystics fail to acknowledge the limitations of introspection. Looking into your own mind will tell you about your own mind and ONLY about your own mind. How can studying your own mind tell you what exists outside of your own mind? It can't, because introspection, by its very nature, is limited to your own mind.

Now you can make some educated guesses based on various inferences, but theses are hardly evidence. Rebirth may have been an educated guess by the Buddha based on the worldview of the time. Stephen Bachelor argues that the Buddha was a pragmatist, and the question of rebirth was really a side issue.

Was the Buddha All-Knowing?

A number of traditional Buddhists believe that the Buddha was "omniscient." But he was not. Those who say that "The recluse Gotama claims to be omniscient," the Buddha explains, "misrepresent me with what is untrue and contrary to fact." (MN 71).

He could be, and was, mistaken on what exists. Just realize that the Buddha didn't know what the brain was or did. It is mentioned in passing, but seen simply as that which filled the head (Nip 1.11). You will notice that the brain is not included in the contemplation of the body in the Satipatthana Sutta (MN 10). The Thai tradition, however, added it later. Overlooking the most complex thing in the known universe is a pretty big oversight.

Consciousness

Those who believe in rebirth usually say that it is the consciousness that is reborn, that transmigrates from one body to another. But science has reached the conclusion that, given the current evidence, consciousness does not exist outside the brain.

The online dictionary Merriam-Webster.com defines consciousness as, "the condition of being conscious : the normal state of being awake and able to understand what is happening around you : a person's mind and thoughts : knowledge that is shared by a group of people."

The Mind is What the Brain Does

Working with the above definition, we know that it is the brain that makes us "able to understand what is happening around" us. The mind is what the brain does. Eliminate the brain and the mind ceases.

This is why that if you injure the brain, you change a person's consciousness. Give him or her drugs, and you alter their consciousness. The only way this can be the case is if the brain and consciousness are deeply intertwined, to the point of being indistinguishable.

A Make-Believe World

The believer in rebirth must retreat to the safe ground of theology and philosophy, where evidence is found in religious texts, spiritual gurus, and subjective personal experiences. It is here that they create a make-believe world of the metaphysical.

In this make-believe world, they say that science cannot make any claim on whether or not consciousness is a metaphysical entity. This is not true. Neuroscientists are generally agreed that consciousness is a natural phenomenon based on the brain. The problem they are working on is how the brain creates consciousness.

Theories of Consciousness

And there are theories out there. For example, Michael Graziano, professor of neuroscience at Princeton University, has published a book called *Consciousness and the Social Brain*. In it he explains his theory about how the brain generates consciousness.

Advocates of rebirth want consciousness to be a metaphysical philosophical question. Why? Because then they can make the leap of faith, and they don't need to rely on real evidence. They don't want science to answer the question, because they don't like the answer. So they have to move the question from the field of science to the field of philosophy.

Not Automatically Metaphysical

I might also add that just because something is unknown, doesn't mean that it is automatically a "metaphysical" question. You cannot just jump to the assumption that consciousness is metaphysical. You must first prove that consciousness is not physical, and then you are welcome to make that move.

But as I have said, the brain and consciousness work as one. When my brain gets drunk, my consciousness is directly affected. When I get a brain injury, it affects my consciousness. Split my brain in half and I literally have two consciousnesses (Sam Harris, 2014). This is not a mild correlation, but a cause and effect relationship.

Name Calling

And if all their pseudo-evidence doesn't work, they resort to just calling me names. This is so juvenile. When they can't actually prove their point, the next best thing is to start calling the other person's ideas "ridiculous" or "naive" or "uncritical." Now I am not sure how all this fits in with Right Speech. They claim, after all, to be Buddhists.

It is not like I go to the websites or YouTube channels of those who believe in rebirth and argue with them. I honor the Buddha's teaching that each of us is to be our own refuge. That means each of us has a right and responsibility for our own spiritual path. Nowhere does the Buddha instruct his disciples to go around correcting other teachers.

The Buddha only gives correction and instruction when asked. Those who claim to follow the Buddha would do good to actually follow the Buddha's example.

But what really bothers these Buddhist fundamentalists, is that I claim to be a Buddhist. They just can't believe that someone would approach Buddhism from a critical and skeptical perspective, and still have the audacity to call themselves a Buddhist, albeit a secular Buddhist.

Secular Buddhist

To them, Buddhism just doesn't make any sense without multiple life karma and rebirth. To them, I am sure that is true. And that is fine, they can have their Buddhism with rebirth. I will even go so far are to argue that the Buddha seems to agree with them. But I don't. I am not a traditional Buddhist, I am a Secular Buddhist. The Buddha was a product of his culture, time, and worldview.

What About Nirvana?

Why spend so much time and effort trying to attain Nirvana then, if rebirth is not true? Of course, I am not trying to attain freedom from rebirth, I am aiming to end suffering for myself and for all the inhabitants of this world. I believe this would be a worthy goal in the Buddha's eyes.

The Buddha said that his aim was to end suffering. That is the point. A hedonist is dedicated to stirring up the very things that cause suffering for oneself and for all sentient beings. Furthermore, since I don't believe in rebirth, it follows that, if I am right, then I have no further rebirths. Rather my concern is the results of my life and actions on the planet I leave behind. I want to leave positive and beneficial fruits for those that come after me.

And they always come back to the claim that you can't be a Buddhist without believing in rebirth. Says who? Do we now have a Buddhist Pope? There is no central authority in Buddhism higher than oneself.

The Buddha wasn't a Buddhist

First of all, the Buddha wasn't a Buddhist. Therefore, there are no requirements to be a Buddhist. Buddhism was created by modern scholars to speak about the Buddha Dharma, or the Way of the Buddha. Therefore, a Buddhist is someone who practices the Way of the Buddha.

This would include following the general teachings of the Buddha. There are numerous different branches of Buddhism and they have many disagreements. What they all generally agree on is the Four Nobles Truths, the Eightfold Noble Path, and the Three Marks of Existence.

Since I agree with these, I am a Buddhist and I don't need anybody's permission to call myself a Buddhist. If someone doesn't like it, they can report me to the Buddhist Vatican and have me excommunicated.

Oh wait, there is no such thing. You know why? Because the Buddha wasn't interested in controlling what others believed. He was interested in showing people a path of practice they could do, one that would allow them to see for themselves the cause of suffering and become free from it.

October 24, 2015, Blog

11

REBIRTH, NATURALISM, AND EVIDENCE

How do I respond when someone uses James Leininger as evidence of reincarnation?

It is the story of a little boy who is said to be the reincarnation of an American World War II pilot who the Japanese shot down and killed. There is also the work of Ian Stevenson.

Someone might ask, how is it that neither is evidence? To them, it might appear that I am a victim of scientism or materialism.

James Leininger

But I am neither a believer in scientism or materialism. The simple fact is that neither the story of James Leininger, nor the work of Ian Stevenson prove reincarnation, or rebirth for that matter.

Believers in rebirth are credulous. Credulous means that they are "ready to believe especially on slight or uncertain evidence" (Merriam-Webster.com). People using the James Leininger story as "evidence," haven't bothered to check the facts of the story. If they did, they would know that most accounts fail to mention that the boy had visited the World War II Air Museum. Which means the boy would have had able information to dream up a story. Just like Joseph Smith did when he dreamed up the book of Mormon.

So the evidence in the James Leininger story is uncertain at best (Skeptico. 2005). Do you know why people don't research the story, but just believe it? Because they already made up their mind. This is called confirmation bias, looking at the evidence to support what you have already decided is true. "My mind is made up, don't confuse me with the facts." And, as the *Internet Encyclopedia of Philosophy* (2015) states, "Using the Fallacy of Confirmation Bias is often a sign that one has adopted some belief dogmatically and isn't willing to confirm or disconfirm the belief."

Naturalism

For clarification, I am not a materialist, I am a naturalist. As Patrick Hurley (1988, 617) states, "Every scientific experiment is a question the experimenter asks of the world, and the result of that experiment is nature's reply."

You know what is amazing, of all the millions of questions we have asked nature, not once has it given us a supernatural answer. Clearly the evidence is in naturalism's favor.

On ontological questions, religions tells us all kinds of different stories about realms, and beings, and gods. No two agree. That is because religions cannot answer ontological questions (questions of what exists). Only science can answer questions of what exists. We know the atom exists because of experimentation.

Most scientists are not materialists, they are

naturalists. Naturalism is "the view of the world that takes account only of natural elements and forces, excluding the supernatural or spiritual" (Dictionary.com). That is because there is no evidence that anything other than nature exists. It's not that the supernatural cannot exist, it is only that there is no evidence that it does. We have to operate in the light we have, and that light says that all that exists is nature. The burden of proof is on the supernaturalists to demonstrate otherwise.

Ian Stevenson

Whenever people try to prove reincarnation, they bring up the work of Ian Stevenson. But as RationalWiki (2013) point out, "Stevenson thought the best evidence for reincarnation was parent's anecdotal stories concerning children's anecdotal remarks."

In fact, that is all the so called evidence rebirth believers can muster. It's no better. or any more credible, than infomercials or religious testimonies of dreams and visions. The person having these hallucinations and fantasy trips can believe them, but for us mere mortals, we are left to doubt.

One of the problems with Ian Stevenson's work is that he believed in reincarnation, and then set out to prove it. As Richard Rockley (2002) points out, "his belief in reincarnation leads him to miss the obvious explanations for things." The fact is, in the words of Robert T. Carroll (2013), "there seem to be alternative, non-paranormal, explanations for all of his data." The presumption is on the side of naturalism.

Leap of Faith

But if someone is credulous, and they already

have faith in something, it is easy to make the leap of blind faith. This mindset is very familiar to me. There are millions of people just like this. It seems that most religious people tend to kiss their brains good-bye when they "find God." They convert to a religion and then swallow everything it says.

Mere Supposition

Buddhists are no different, even though the Buddha said, "Do not accept anything on mere hearsay. Do not accept anything by mere tradition. Do not accept anything on account of rumours. Do not accept anything just because it accords with your scriptures. Do not accept anything by mere supposition. Do not accept anything by mere inference. Do not accept anything by merely considering the appearances. Do not accept anything merely because it agrees with your preconceived notions. Do not accept anything merely because it seems acceptable. Do not accept anything thinking that the ascetic is respected by us. But when you know for yourselves – these things are immoral, these things are blameworthy, these things are censured by the wise, these things, when performed and undertaken, conduce to ruin and sorrow – then reject them. When you know for yourselves – these things are moral, these things are blameless, these things are praised by the wise, these things, when performed and undertaken, conduce to well-being and happiness – then live and act accordingly" (Kalama Sutta translated by Narada Mahathera).

Those that argue with me about rebirth fail to realize that they are not following the Buddha's teachings or example. Nowhere do you find the Buddha forcing his view on to others. You don't see him arguing with people. If you really understood Buddhism, you would know that attachment to views, even right views, is always a hindrance (Dutthatthaka Sutta). Yet they continue to harass me with their unproven view. This is proof that they are attached to their view.

Attachment to Views

Listen, I am not going to be convinced by anything less than real evidence. But they won't let it go. Many will continue to comment. Do you want to know why?

First, it is because they are attached to views. They can't stand it that someone doesn't believe as they do. Why does it matter? It is all about attachment.

The second reason is because they are actually insecure about their belief in rebirth. They are not trying to convince me, they are trying to convince themselves. The reason it is so important to convince me is that, if they can convince me, then it just confirms their view. In other words, they want to argue, not to discover the truth, but to convince themselves that they already have the truth.

December 2, 2015, Blog

12

NO-SELF AND REBIRTH

In Buddhism, the term anatta (Pali) or anatman (Sanskrit) refers to the view that the self is an illusion. To quote from *The Princeton Dictionary of Buddhism* under the entry *anatman,* it says, "In Sanskrit, 'no self.'"

Now some people make a big distinction between no-self and not-self. They claim that the Buddha didn't teach no-self, but rather not-self.

No-Self and Not-Self
I think that both are true. There is no-self, that is, the self does not exist, rather what exists is the convergence of five aggregates. And likewise, the five aggregates are not-self.

The Self Does Not Exist
What it doesn't mean is that what we identify as the self does not exist, rather, it means that we have misidentified what exists. We have given it attributes that, if we look closely, it does not inherently have. Namely, the self is not a separate entity from everything else. The self is not a permanent, unchanging thing. The self is not the

source of happiness and ultimate freedom.

The Soul

All these misconceptions about the self can be expressed by the word soul. We do not have a soul. We have an ego, but not a soul. An ego is a mental construct that evolved because of its survival benefit. Ego is the brain's ability to construct a mental map of reality. This map of reality created the useful illusion that the conceptual universe revolved around itself. It was the sun to its mental solar system.

Mental Fabrication

The Buddha discovered the reality of these mental fabrications and deconstructed it. By doing so, he discovered the cause of unhappiness and its cure. The mental construct of ego removes us from reality and creates a world of suffering. Eliminate the self, and you eliminate the suffering.

This also means that "you" don't really exist. At least not as you conceive of yourself. Rather, you are just the universe being conscious of itself. To use Carl Sagan's words, "Because the cosmos is also within us. We're made of star-stuff. We are a way for the cosmos to know itself."

Like a Wave

So we exist like a wave on the ocean. From the ocean of the Cosmos we arise, appear to be separate for a while, and then plunge back into the ocean from which we came. In one sense, we never die because we were never born. Yet, in another sense, we exist but for a moment. "What is your life? For you are a mist that appears for a little while and then vanishes" (James 4:14 NRSV).

Rebirth

Now how does this relate to rebirth? Since there is no abiding entity known as a soul or self, and since all the aggregates are impermanent, and hence subject to passing away, what passes from one life to the other? If you say consciousness, then I would ask, "It is impermanent?" Since all conditioned things are impermanent, you have to say yes. But if consciousness changes, how and when does it pass away?

So it is not a matter of whether or not consciousness passes away, but when it does. Traditional Buddhists would say that it passes away at Nirvana. What then exists, since consciousness passes away? Nothing, right? I would argue that consciousness is impermanent and, therefore, passes away at death. There is no existence of "you" after death.

December 9, 2015, Blog

13

PSYCHOLOGICAL KARMA

Karma literally means "action," but the Buddha specifically said that it dealt with intention (AN 6.63). Action can deal with mental or physical phenomenon, but intention is exclusively mental. Karma, therefore, dealt with psychological dynamics.

Metaphysical karma then deals with the belief that your negative actions somehow flow from one life to another through rebirth. Understanding karma without the metaphysical baggage, we could see this happening not through rebirth but through the influences we leave behind. In order words, our actions and even DNA leave lasting effects on the world.

Psychological karma means that our intentional actions shape our minds and lives. It is not mere action that shapes our character and personality, but only our intentional actions. This is because they are willful and become habituated through repetition.

What we sow in our words, thoughts, and deeds, mold and shape the person we are becoming. Here the real danger of delusion is evident. We must become aware of the negative things we think, say, and do in order to redirect them into positive channels. We must wake up to what we do.

September 23, 2015, Blog

14

PSYCHOLOGICAL SAMSARA

Today I want to talk about psychological Samsara. I specify psychological Samsara to distinguish it from metaphysical Samsara. Traditional Buddhism believes that we are caught in a cycle of rebirth, that we do not die but are reborn over and over again until we are enlightened and attain Nirvana.

This is what I am calling metaphysical Samsara, because it asserts things beyond the verifiable evidence of scientific investigation. The Buddha taught it, so I am not saying it's impossible.

What I am saying is that there is no evidence for this, and, to paraphrase the Buddha, "Don't blindly believe what I say. Don't believe me because others convince you of my words. Find out for yourself what is the truth, what is real." As Secular Buddhists, we stick with the evidence and so do not believe in rebirth. But there is a psychological Samsara and I want to discuss this.

The Meaning

First, psychological Samsara is literally the wanderings. The aimlessness of most people's life is very evident. They wander from one job to another, from one spouse to another, and even from one religion to another.

I know psychological Samsara because I have lived there all my life. I have felt like an unanchored boat that has lost its moaring and is aimlessly adrift at sea. All of life is in a state of flux, just like the sea.

People come, people leave, but the churning of life never stops, never eases up. I have lost a father, a sister, and all my grandparents. I have had a number of jobs and have lived many different places. To me, life seems like a wandering, a drifting on the ocean of circumstances.

It is hard not to feel lost, disoriented, and confused. We want something solid, something sure, something lasting. Many grasp for hope in religion, where we are promised something solid, something sure, something lasting. The only catch is, that this solidity is in another world beyond this one. Fortunately or unfortunately, some of us actually look at the evidence for this other world and find it lacking at best.

Out of Ignorance

Second, psychological Samsara arises out of ignorance. This psychological lostness and hence our endless wandering arises out of ignorance. Ignorance in Buddhism means the failure to see the facts of life as they are.

We do not see ourselves as we really are, nor do we conduct ourselves in harmony with these realities. The three characteristics of existence expose three of the most glaring mistakes we make about reality.

The first is that we think we can find something permanent in a world where everything is impermanent. Constant flux is the essential nature of reality, looking for something unchangeable and permanent is futile. Yet we hate change, even though that is the very nature of our existence. Hating the inevitable is a waste of time and emotional energy. Just accept it. It's not going to change just because you don't.

The second characteristic of existence is that of no-self. There is no abiding and enduring self, you are a part of this flux. Any fixity from one moment to another is caused by the flow of cause and effect, action and habit.

Suffering and Dissatisfaction

The third characteristic is that life is suffering, and that is our third point. Psychological Samsara is characterized by suffering and dissatisfaction.

Since we completely misread reality and the way things really are, we suffer. We suffer because we are attached to ideas, to people, to places, and to things. In the sea of impermanence all is in flux, all will change, all will end.

Yet this is not what we believe because this is not how we act. We do not act like tomorrow is completely uncertain, yet it is. We act as if we will have a tomorrow, but we don't know that.

We furthermore act as if our relationships will last forever. I never had a chance to say goodbye to my Dad or my sister, they just slipped away one day. Your parents and siblings will too one day.

Don't live as if you have a tomorrow, live fully in the present moment. Samsara is wandering, stop wandering. Anchor yourself in the flow of the present moment, the only reality that is real.

In conclusion, psychological Samsara is the mental and emotional lostness that we all feel and can be seen in the way we wander aimlessly through life. Psychological Samsara is caused, not by anything we did wrong, but being unaware of the way reality really is beneath the surface of appearances. And this ignorance leads to attachments and aversions, and ultimately to suffering and dissatisfaction.

September 18, 2015, Podcast

15

PSYCHOLOGICAL NIRVANA

Today I want to talk about Nirvana, psychological Nirvana. I specify psychological Nirvana to distinguish it from metaphysical nirvana. Nirvana is one of Buddhism's most misunderstood terms.

To many people, Nirvana is kind of like heaven, a place you go to after death. Of course, this is not what Nirvana means. In fact, the Buddha entered Nirvana on the day he was enlightened.

At his death, the Pali Canon says he entered Parinirvana, meaning Nirvana-after-death. Most schools of Buddhism explain Nirvana as a state that may be experienced in life, or it may be entered into at death.

This metaphysical Nirvana was believed to occur upon the death of the body of someone who had attained Nirvana during their lifetime. Since no two schools of Buddhism seem to agree on every aspect of this metaphysical Nirvana, I want to focus on understanding psychological Nirvana.

The End of Suffering

First, psychological Nirvana is the end of suffering. The First Noble Truth is that life is filled with suffering. The Second Noble Truth is that the cause of suffering is attachment. And the Third Noble Truth is that suffering can come to an end through ending attachment.

This ending of suffering and dissatisfaction is called Nirvana in Buddhism. Since the suffering and dissatisfaction is psychological rather than physical, the Nirvana is psychological rather than physical, or metaphysical, as in the case of an afterlife.

So Nirvana is the psychological state of the ceasing of suffering and dissatisfaction. Another way to say it is that Nirvana is inner freedom and deep contentment. It is a psychological state characterized by bliss or inner peace.

This is the goal of Buddhism, the end of suffering and dissatisfaction. The goal is not going to heaven, but finding true happiness in this life - this bliss or inner peace.

Blowing Out

Second, psychological Nirvana is the blowing out of the three fires. The word Nirvana literally means "to blow out." The Buddha taught that the cause of suffering and dissatisfaction was the three poisons, namely attachment, aversion, and delusion. They are also known as fires, because of their ability to spread and their causing of mental and emotional pain.

Nirvana, then, is the blowing out of the fires of attachment, aversion, and delusion. When they are completely extinguished the result is freedom, peace, contentment, and bliss.

This is true happiness, and Buddhism teaches that it can be found in this life. Everyone has the desire to be happy and avoid suffering. Only Buddhism has found a way to make it happen.

Admittedly, for most of us, Buddhism doesn't provide us with unending happiness. But it does lessen our suffering and make life more meaningful and happy. How far we are freed from suffering and dissatisfaction depends on how free we are from attachment, aversion, and delusion.

And how far we are freed from attachment, aversion, and delusion, depends upon on how far we get on the Eightfold Noble Path. And how far we get on the Eightfold Noble Path depends on how diligent we are in practice and how open we are to compassionate action and wise living. Like guitar strings, our practice must not be too loose or too tight. Simplicity, balance, and moderation are the ways of the wise.

The Buddha's Main Concern

Third, psychological Nirvana was the Buddha's main concern. In the prescientific culture of India, reincarnation or rebirth was a given. It was believed that people keep reincarnating until they were reabsorbed back into God.

The Buddha revised this belief by eliminating the soul in the equation. He rightly came to the conclusion that there was no abiding self, and hence, no soul. What then continues from one existence to another, what then is reincarnated or reborn?

This has never been agreed upon by Buddhists. The usual theories deal with the stream of consciousness that somehow transfers from one body to another. But this makes consciousness appear to be some kind of abiding entity, which is contrary to the Buddha's teachings.

Luckily for us, it doesn't matter, because metaphysical Nirvana will take care of itself. If you reach Nirvana in this life, you automatically get ultimate Nirvana at death, whatever that turns out to be.

In conclusion, we all want to be free from suffering and dissatisfaction. The Third Noble Truth tells us that this wish is possible and it is called Nirvana. Wanting to be happy is the same thing as wanting Nirvana. Nirvana is the ultimate happiness where we are free from suffering and dissatisfaction and live in a state of bliss and inner peace. I think this is a goal worth dedicating our lives to.

September 11, 2015, Podcast

16

METAPHYSICAL NIRVANA

In my last chapter I distinguished psychological Nirvana from metaphysical Nirvana. Psychological Nirvana deals with the state of bliss and inner peace when the fires of attachment, aversion, and delusion are blown out.

The Buddha entered psychological Nirvana on the day he was enlightened. Metaphysical Nirvana was believed to occur upon the death of the body of someone who had attained psychological Nirvana during their lifetime, or at their death.

Nirvana is usually translated as "extinction," but this doesn't catch the real meaning. Extinction carries the ideal that the person is annihilated. But in Buddhism there is not an abiding self, no soul, and hence, nothing to be annihilated.

Stream of Consciousness

Most schools of Buddhism teach that it is the stream of consciousness that survivals death and is reborn until a person reaches enlightenment. But meditation will show you that consciousness is undefiled, it is like a mirror. The taints do not exist in consciousness, but in habituated habits of mind and attitude.

In the prescientific culture of India, it was believed that people keep reincarnating until they are reabsorbed back into Brahma. The Buddha revised this belief by rejecting the idea of a soul. But what then is reborn if there is no abiding soul?

The usual proposed solutions deal with the stream of consciousness that somehow transfers from one body to another. But this makes consciousness appear to be some kind of abiding entity, which is contrary to the Buddha's teachings.

Give Up Rebirth

I think it is better to just give up the idea of rebirth of anything other than the consequences of our words and actions.

Nothing lasts forever, all things end. We end with the death of our brain. This is the most consistent hypothesis with both the Buddha's teaching of no-self and the latest findings of neuroscience. It is, therefore, the most reasonable conclusion based on the evidence.

September 14, 2015, Blog

17

THERE IS NO BUDDHISM WITHOUT BELIEFS

Let's begin with a simple question. What is a belief? A belief is simply a claim we accept as true. And a claim is a statement that is either true or false. So if someone makes a statement that we accept as true, we have a belief.

So does Buddhism makes statements that people accept? Of course, many of them. Can we practice Buddhism without believing anything Buddhist?

Buddhism Without Beliefs

Well, Stephen Batchelor claims we can have Buddhism without beliefs, which is actually a title of one of his books. I enjoyed the book, but I am not sure such a thing is really possible.

I often hear that Buddhism is not a belief system. This is absolutely not true. Buddhism is a belief system just as much as Christianity, Hinduism, and Zoroastrianism. You can't live life without believing things.

The difference is that Buddhism has the least amount of metaphysical baggage, and the metaphysical baggage is not essential to the philosophy or practice of the Buddha.

Now if you said you can have Buddhism without metaphysical beliefs, then yes, such is possible. But every philosophy, including Humanism, has beliefs ("Humanism believes," Humanist Manifesto I).

Four Wise Beliefs

The Four Noble Truths, which might better be called the Four Wise Beliefs, form the core of Buddhism's belief system. Belief one, all people suffer and are dissatisfied. Belief two, the cause of suffering and dissatisfaction is reactivity. Belief three, reactivity can be eliminated. Belief four, the Eightfold Noble Path can eliminate reactivity and hence suffering and dissatisfaction.

The Four Tasks

Now do the Four Wise Beliefs stop being beliefs to be accepted, if they are turned into tasks to be accomplished? Stephen Batchelor turned the Four Noble Truths into the Four Tasks. First, fully know suffering. Second, let go of craving or reactivity. Third, experience the cessation of craving. and four, cultivate the eightfold path.

The first task is to fully know suffering. Why? Yes, it is a task. But it is a task without a reason to pursue it. Stand on your head. Why? Because I said so. See, it makes no sense to issue a task without a reason to so the task.

Why Embrace Suffering

So why should we embrace suffering? Because suffering is bad (a belief) and unnecessary (another belief). So the first task assumes, at least two beliefs, first that suffering is a bad thing that we should not want. And second, that suffering is, at least to some extent, unnecessary. In other words, we don't have to suffer.

So you can't have Buddhist practice without believing, or at least assuming, Buddhist beliefs. Otherwise, you have a task without a reason, a practice without a purpose, and a meditation without an objective.

And before someone objects that you shouldn't meditate with a goal, remember that you started meditating for a reason. Why? That is, or at least was, your objective.

Personally, I think it is quite alright to see the Four Noble Truths as four foundational beliefs to Buddhist practice. In fact, I think this is the most rational and logical way to see them.

Doctor Treating a Patient

The Four Wise Beliefs are similar to a doctor diagnosing and treating a patient. The First Belief is the diagnosis of a problem, humanity is unhappy and dissatisfied. This has been empirically verified, and you can see if it's true in your life as well. Science says the first belief is true.

The Second Belief is concerning the cause of the illness. The Buddha taught that the cause of unhappiness was reactivity, which takes three forms, attachment, aversion, and ignorance. Is the Buddha right? We can judge this by personal experience or we can see its truth in the latest findings of Psychology. Science says the second belief is probably true.

The Third Belief is the that there is a cure. The jury is still out on whether we can only lessen suffering or whether we can completely cure it. We cannot be dogmatic either way. We can only say what works for us. Science says the third belief is probably true, at least to some extent.

The Fourth Belief is the prescription. This is the "how to" part. It involves forming wise views, wise intentions, wise speech, wise action, wise livelihood, wise effort, wise mindfulness, and wise concentration. Science says the fourth belief is producing results in the lives of millions.

A Healthy Dose of Skepticism

So is Stephen Batchelor wrong? I prefer to see him as a finger pointing at the moon. We need to come to Buddhism with skepticism and a desire to live an evidence-based life.

The evidence is in favor of Buddhism's core principles. Whether it is the complete story, I am not so sure.

So can we have Buddhism without any beliefs? No. But we can have a secularized Buddhist practice without the metaphysical baggage. And that, I believe, is the spirit of what Stephen is getting at.

March 28, 2016, Blog

ONLINE RESOURCES

- **Secular Buddhist Association**
  http://secularbuddhism.org/
- **Secular Buddhism Australia**
  http://www.secularbuddhism.org.au/
- **Säkularer Buddhismus (Austria)**
  http://www.saekularerbuddhismus.org/
- **Secular Buddhism (Canada)**
  http://secularbuddhism.wordpress.com/
- **Centro Meditazione Roma (Italy)**
  http://www.centromeditazioneroma.it/
- **Secular Buddhism New Zealand (New Zealand)**
  http://secularbuddhism.org.nz/
- **Secular Sangha (Scotland)**
  http://www.secularsangha.org/
- **Budismo Secular (Spain)**
  http://www.budismosecular.org/
- **Sekulär Buddhism (Sweden)**
  http://sekularbuddhism.wordpress.com/
- **Secular Buddhism U.K.**
  http://www.secularbuddhism.co.uk/
- **Martine and Stephen Batchelor**
  http://www.stephenbatchelor.org/

BIBLIOGRAPHY

Asma, Stephen T. 2011. *Why I Am a Buddhist: No-Nonsense Buddhism for Modern Living*. London: Watkins, 2011.

Batchelor, Stephen. 2015. *After Buddhism: Rethinking the Dharma for a Secular Age*. New Haven, CT: Yale University Press.

Bateman, Rick. 2010. *Secular Buddhism: No Robes, No Ritual, No Religion*. Posted July 4, 2010. Accessed April 17, 2016. http://secularbuddhism.wordpress.com/

Blackmore, Sue. 2008. "Back from the grave." *The Guardian*. Published September 19, 2008. Accessed August 14, 2015. http://www.theguardian.com/commentisfree/2008/sep/19/health.mentalhealth

Bodhi, Bhikkhu, trans. 2000. *The Connected Discourses of the Buddha: A Translation of the Samyutta Nikaya*. Boston: Wisdom Publication.

Bodhi, Bhikkhu, trans. 2012. *The Numerical Discourses of the Buddha: A Translation of the Anguttara Nikaya*. Boston: Wisdom Publication.

Carroll, Robert T. 2013. "Ian Stevenson (1918-2007)." *Skeptic's Dictionary*. December 23, 2013. Accessed December 2, 2015. http://skepdic.com/stevenson.html

Conze, Edward, trans. 1959. *Buddhist Scriptures*. New York: Penguin Books.

Dowden, Bradley. 2015. "Fallacies." *Internet Encyclopedia of Philosophy*. Accessed December 2, 2015. http://www.iep.utm.edu/fallacy/

Edelglass, William and Jay L. Garfield, eds. 2009. *Buddhist Philosophy: Essential Readings*. New York: Oxford University Press.

Flanagan, Owen. 2011. *The Bodhisattva's Brain: Buddhism Naturalized*. Cambridge, MA: MIT Press.

Grayling, A. c. 2013. *The God Argument: Te Case Against Religion and for Humanism*. New York: Bloomsbury.

Gura, Mark W. 2015. *Exploring Your Life:*

Mindfulness Meditation and Secular Spirituality. Duluth, GA: InnerAction Press.

Guruge, Ananda W. P. and K G Amaradasa. 1956. "Kalama Sutta," 2500 Buddha Jayanti. Colombo: Buddhist Council of Ceylon.

Gyatso, Geshe Kelsang. 1993. *Introduction to Buddhism*. London: Tharpa Publications.

Hurley, Patrick J. 1988. *A Concise Introduction to Logic*. Belmont, CA: Wadsworth.

Lama, Dalai. 2005. *The Universe in a Single Atom: The Convergence of Science and Spirituality*. New York: Broadway Books.

Life of the Buddha for Secondary Students. 2002. Buddha Dharma Education Association. Accessed December 17, 2015. http://www.buddhanet.net/pdf_file/a4lifebuddha.pdf.

McMahan, David L. 2008. *The Making of Buddhist Modernism*. New York: Oxford University Press.

Mendis, N.K.G. 2006. "The Abhidhamma in Practice," *Access to Insight* (Legacy Edition). Accessed December 17, 2015. http://www.accesstoinsight.org/lib/authors/mendis/wheel322.html.

Nanamoli, Bhikkhu and Bhikkhu Bodhi, trans. 2009. *The Middle Length Discourses of the*

Buddha: A Translation of the Majjhima Nikaya. Boston: Wisdom Publication.

Nhat Hanh, Thich. 1993. *Interbeing: Fourteen Guidelines for Engaged Buddhism*. Berkeley, CA: Parallax Press.

Nhat Hanh, Thich. 1995. *Zen Keys*. New York: Three Leaves Press.

Rahula, Walpola. 1974. *What the Buddha Taught*. New York: Grove Press.

Rasheta, Noah. 2016. *Secular Buddhism: A Modern Take on Ancient Wisdom*. Posted January 4, 2016. Accessed April 17, 2016. http://secularbuddhism.com/what-is-secular-buddhism/

RationalWiki. 2013. "Ian Stevenson." *RationalWiki*. November 10, 2013. Accessed December 2, 2015. http://rationalwiki.org/wiki/Ian_Stevenson

Rockley, Richard. 2002. "The apparent belief system of Ian Stevenson." *Skeptic Report*. October 1, 2002. Accessed December 2, 2015. http://www.skepticreport.com/sr/?p=481

Sagan, Carl. 1996. *The Demon-Haunted World: Science as a Candle in the Dark*. New York: Ballantine Books.

Skeptico. 2005. "Reincarnation all over again."

Skeptico. July 07, 2005. Accessed December 2, 2015. http://skeptico.blogs.com/skeptico/2005/07/reincarnation_a.html

Snelling, John. 1998. *The Buddhist Handbook: A complete Guide to Buddhist Teaching and Practice*. London: Rider.

Vessantara. 2004. *Meeting the Buddhas: A Guide to Buddhas, Bodhisattvas, and Tantric Deities*. Windhorse Publications.

Walshe, Maurice, trans. 1995. *The Long Discourses of the Buddha: A Translation of the Digha Nikaya*. Boston: Wisdom Publication. and world."

ABOUT THE AUTHOR

Jay N. Forrest is a Humanist Meditation Teacher. He is an ordained Humanist Celebrant and a member of the American Humanist Association. Jay is also a Certified Meditation Teacher, having been trained in both Zen and Vipassana meditation practices.

Before becoming a nontheist and a Humanist, Jay was a Pentecostal Evangelical Pastor for over two decades. He was a Christian minister with several denominations, including The International Pentecostal Holiness Church. Jay did his undergraduate work at Central Bible College and Berean University, and received his Doctorate of Ministry from Trinity Evangelical Christian University.

Jay is the author of seven books, including his best-selling book, *Practical Buddhism: Wisdom for Everyday Life*. He has written hundreds of articles for websites, newspapers, and magazines such as The Houston Chronicle, Be Still Magazine, The Cutting Edge, Patheos, and is a contributing writer for the Spiritual

Naturalist Society.

Jay is the host of the Jay Forrest Show (formerly called 5 Minute Dharma). The show features enlightening and informative interviews helping people discover their own wisdom path. The Show has had more than 300,000 downloads and can be found on iTunes, Stitcher, TuneIn, and YouTube. Jay has also appeared as a guest on other podcasts including The Secular Buddhist Podcast, The Next Half by Tony Russell, Living Your Yoga TV, and others.

Jay's main interests are in philosophy, psychology, and religion. Much of his writing deals with the philosophy and ethics of secular Humanism and the teachings and meditation practices of secular Buddhism. Other interests include Positive Psychology, Humanistic Psychology, Cognitive Behavioral Therapy, Religious Naturalism, Neuroscience, Meteorology, and Physics.

Printed in Great Britain
by Amazon